Praise for
Bachelor

Gustavo Hernandez, it would be my honor if you would school me on how to write the modern love poem. *Bachelor* is a once-in-a-lifetime book that transcends the sensations of physical touch, deep-eyed stares, and late-night whispers from the greatest lovers. Somewhere the moon is tucked away watching. Somewhere I am licking an orange rind as the California sun rises, and I am reminded of the power I hold over a past lover. *This* is the power Hernandez's speaker bestows on his readers. It is the gift of wisdom—of having lived *and* living every moment through the sensory and synesthetic—through the sensational and sensual—through the impossible and divine. *Again*. Man. Son. Lover. Uncle. Boyfriend. Volta. Hunk. Sunset. *Again*. Hernandez's work is the scent association of musk and vanilla dancing in nostalgia as his speakers reach the ineffable realm of longing. Oh, Gustavo Hernandez, thank you for teaching us longing. Thank you for teaching us *passion*. Take us into the nocturne. After all, aren't all the greatest people on Earth, bachelors?

—**Dorothy Chan**, author of
Babe and *Return of the Chinese Femme*

Gustavo Hernandez writes from the slippery threshold between the living and the dead, from "The last table before the dance floor." These poems inhabit places-that-are, and then transfigure into places-that-once-were, like the *Cienega*, a swampland once inhabited by singing tree frogs, land tamed by "the hands and blades and bricks of ghosts," and Jalisco, the mother/fatherland, where his morning run *here,* in Santa Ana, is also a "race from our plaza to the western borders of Tototlan." Indeed, the poems' speaker moves like a ghost, from affiliation to singularity and back again, from son, brother, uncle, lover, to a state of profound bachelorhood, a traveler moving through a house of mirrors who encounters and re-encounters himself. These are poems that Hernandez choreographs around a seed of stillness and silence, poems with the elegance of Meche Barba in a black and white film, who "dances under a white perfumy pseudonym." Theirs is the syntax of the dead. Theirs is the understanding that nothing is just one thing; they "reject reduction" at every turn. Maybe that is why so many poems in this collection share the same title— "Bachelor," "Husband," "Nocturne," "Son," "I Can't Settle on One Figure for a Sunset," "Conclusion," from mirror to mirror, an archetype turned in the hand like a cut diamond, each poem, a facet. In *Bachelor,* Hernandez has written a book like no other, inhabited by poems of the soul.

—**Diane Seuss**, author of
frank: sonnets and *Modern Poetry*

This myth, like everything/ else in the realm of love," Gustavo Hernandez writes in *Bachelor,* "can be stripped down to the vulnerable." Hernandez's poetry superpowers are lyric vulnerability and the ability to strip a narrative down to its essences. In his poetic lexicon, bachelorhood is not a descriptor as much as it is a mindset, an ability to name the world's loneliness, then keep it company. The lines between bachelor and husband, between living and dead, between family and neighbor, "can be blurred" and, "if necessary, expanded." *Bachelor* will seduce you: "lonely doesn't have to mean lonely anymore."

—**James Allen Hall**, author of
Romantic Comedy

BACHELOR

FLOWERSONG
PRESS

poetry by

GUSTAVO HERNANDEZ

FLOWERSONG
PRESS

FlowerSong Press
Copyright © 2025 by Gustavo Hernandez
ISBN: 978-1-963245-89-9

Published by FlowerSong Press
in the United States of America.
www.flowersongpress.com

Author Photo by Alexis Rhone Fancher

Set in Adobe Garamond Pro

NOTICE: SCHOOLS AND BUSINESSES

FlowerSong Press offers copies of this book at quantity discount with bulk
purchase for educational, business, or sales promotional use. For information,
please email the Publisher at info@flowersongpress.com.

For Casandra, Yuzuko, and Maximiliano

table of contents

BACHELOR

One does not receive proposals of marriage every day in this enlightened age, although curiously enough I have had two this year. I seem to have accepted them both.

—**Anita Brookner,**
Hotel du Lac

BARITONE

What it all sounds like. These steps and the faded bullnose
brick, the guardrail built for my mother. Upstairs, the sky
is curved in a smooth medieval heaven's cloud motif.
A small plane glows orange in this hour where the last
drinks are served and the cabin goes somber. It isn't unpleasant.
Standing here, I am not an unpleasant man. I pray often.
For my young. To anything slow-moving to keep everything slow-
moving, and it is still something to pray, however little action
there is in it. You think and mouth and wait to be acted upon.
And in this waiting, I often stand right here and wonder
about my voice. What it is now. The cloudy painting.
These children. My mother. Me in the third person. Him.
What I can hold—and the way I hold him—in my hands.

CIENEGA

The only thing I learned today is that in this county
there once sloshed a swamp full of tree frogs.

Before drainage channels, in the willows, before the dry heave
of our cowboy airport, was the song, were their throats.
Their public participation a sort of landmark.

We know our fathers were ordered to tame that land and grass, hermano.
Everywhere the hands and blades and bricks of ghosts,
and I want to be real—I'm lost
in the development and reconfiguration. In the dead, hermano.

Everywhere the hands and blades and bricks of ghosts.
Everywhere their lungs, their mouths, and their grown children.

Brother, do you think it's true that we are never just one body?
Brother, did you know the swamp and its unified voice
once helped travelers find their way through the night?

NOCTURNE

The kind where the horses have been hitched to the trees.
Where the granary door's been locked and the money
stashed in the box in the wall. If it's free,
my grandfather used to say, I will take
even a punch to the face. I think that's a misquote,
but that's what I do these days. I mess with the syntax—live
in the belongings—of the dead. My mother goes
to bed, and I'm left to turn the locks in the house, to sit
in the kitchen and survey what's left on the table.
I know there is no way to safeguard what we have.
No bolt that will hold. My grandfather couldn't
have seen himself growing old. His fortune at the mercy
of so many. What happened to the late hope in the rain
rustle of the cypress? The ordered security
of the stacked rocks around the cows and the pasture?
Only now, nearly alone, do I realize how little
of the earth you can take with you. Not the paper
that counts itself whole in my pocket. Not the bread
and milk. Not even the bread and milk
I have in the smudge between night and the morning.

HUSBAND

Despite the times we couldn't decide
how to answer, we went on.

That spring, on the road home
from Arizona, when the thundering sky began
to unseat itself and we felt the desert
in California come up and ask us
for a definition.

I'd realized by then we'd never know
how to pin it down,
what we needed. I—
at that point—just needed you
to join me in saying that

lovers like us want
to be called, to call each other,
different things:

>   Hunk / Honeycomb
>   Heart / Habitat

Things that can be blurred. If necessary, expanded.

DIVORCE WITH PULLED-BACK CURTAIN
AND ELECTRICAL WIRING

Even the neighbors are going through this
with me. Maybe more than the family
I worry or those old, discarded friends
who'd no doubt say I'm suffering
from a tangled spirit, who'd prompt me
to dive into some mystic bog
for a solution, even though they know
I no longer have the eye or the knife
for that. The men next door never prompt
or ask. They regularly slice
plastic away from copper wire
and listen to me moving.
They hear the songs of a romantic,
the machine bolts of a futurist,
the words of someone who fears
the contour that his questions form.
Sometimes there's a poker game. Sometimes
they look away from their hands to see
what my hands and my shampoo have done
to my new boyfriend's dark hair.
Of my progress, I do believe
they have the clearest accounting.
The tones of my voice. The discographies
shifting. The years away from the family home
I cry and shower off. We've thrown away
every bit of the small talk and the posturing.
In the mornings, we wave and watch
our eyes become more earnest by the day.

CONCLUSION

It is that I feel alone.

The rest, you should know, is the rent-a-bed and my keys
next to the television. The whole room if you'd like it.
Orange County winding down outside and dark gray.

Everyone I've been with this spring has felt like something
more than me. God after God.
Gods like the weathermen calling the last arcs of rain.

I've never figured it out.
How to trust myself or predict even one action in the sky.

It is supposed to come down again tonight.
A man undresses in front of me.

From his jacket I can tell the first drops must have fallen
while I was watching him smoke in the parking lot.

HUSBAND

How wrong I'd been to think of the end
as something whole, as something present
only at the tip of a straight line.

Do you remember how I used to make it okay
for us to admit we didn't make use
of the day like we'd promised?

The words I used to describe the city
most nights?

Glimmering / Glinting / Aglitter

For each of those there was a corresponding failure.

A tipped vessel, then light
on the absence of some aquifer of the heart.

I CAN'T SETTLE ON ONE FIGURE
FOR A SUNSET

Though sometimes I'd like for it to be the willow thicket.
The late breeze in the driveway my father said was sea air.
If he were still here, I'd tell him what I've learned
about the salt marshes on the coast. Old hiding place
of outlaws and preachers. I want a sunset to be all of that.
I want to reject reduction. Like a surfer is allowed
to hold beauty and fear in the same hand. On Highway One,
at fourteen, my father taught me about the solstice. Summer
and its lengthening. Time passing. I'm old enough now
to demand a sunset mean something. Old enough
to be granted, not one, but a handful of images.
The thicket. The outlaw. Not the preacher, but his bell.
The bell and my father and the days growing longer.

YUZUKO AT EVENING MASS

What is important, I say to my niece, is the way the cars light up
the stained glass. The gold-tipped dramatics of Saint George.
The cowslip and the Christmas rose. I don't know
what she believes of apostles or virgins or saints,
those who witnessed moon beams in red and blue and thought
God and thought blood and thought baptism. She may,
like me, be taken to task for wanting a nebulous love,
an unfocused peace, unguided by doctrine or scripture.
I rub holy water behind her ear. I do. I hold her hand
on the way to the car, but don't know if I've correctly implored
anyone for the soul of my own mother and father. The moon
is obscured tonight. I guide her face up to the parking lot light.

BAPTISM

for Maximiliano

The night before, I sat outside with you.
In the dark, you wandered out
under the blossoms to the jasmine.
I did not follow. There are corners
of this place that I have sworn off
in my grief. Years ago, I went into the shed
and threw out all my father's shovels.
That is loss: divestment and rigidity. Acting
on a sliver of the moon. For the shovels,
my mother said she would never forgive me.
That, too, is loss. And a lesson.
I introduce you now in what I had
the sense to keep. The jasmine
and the citrus trees. I did not plant them,
but they were entrusted to me.

PAD

Sometimes the walls here are painted hot pink and green
like a set in a Mexican comedy show. Sometimes only hot,
closed off and white like a room in any Chopin story.

The sky outside is dark and rain only a sign to bring
the trousers in. Into this old ghost box where I
mouth my way through some dead play or sitcom rerun.

Where I have learned the word inheritance: the marble
and siding are passed down. The open hands
have given and are now nearly unreachable.

When I dream and ask about the roof and the begonias,
my parents point to my lungs and to my hands.
They place their palms on my temples.

They ask me what I know and what I've learned
how to carry. They ask, and I have learned so little.
I wake with the neighbors' coffee machines.

At this age I still wonder about divine automation.
If today the independent will and movement
of the earth will make me able. If that burden is on me.

BACHELOR

In one of the black and white films my mother watches,
José Venegas plays a man known only as El Bronco.
In black he leads a town into sin through the mouth
of a cabaret. In another film, Meche Barba dances
under a white perfumy pseudonym. The men at her hips
are announced only as her satellites. Hired to smile
and to mimic her movement. Slick and rehearsed.
I tell my mother that is the only way I want to know how to love.
Passion through discipline. The lobby piano.
The note played and the note only suggested. The master
of ceremonies who is paid to describe the night as glossy black,
whose eyes in the last of the glossy black say nothing to you
other than *Ladies and Gentlemen, that was the show.*

HUSBAND

After that night the night no longer cut
like a black, sharpened pendulum.

You were gone,
and it was easy as a story
where the outline of one man
replaces the outline of another.

If you want to know what I remember:

The eaves / The windshield / Dripping

In some dark lot in me, relief.
The cold moon and what I considered
my own unnatural strength returning.

You were gone. It was so clean.
It was too quick. It's brutal. I know.

And the next morning, when I came home
and got her up for breakfast, my mother
said that in her sleep she'd been again
to that white place where all souls go.

Where my father went.
She said it was no dream.

She said it was no dream, and I had to believe her.
How could I doubt her?
In that world warped by absence,
in that after condition.

SON

My father cried the first time he saw me dancing.
Not an early dance. Not a spring dance.
A fall wedding. I was in my thirties. He cried.
That is how far he thought me from that kind of joy.

There are years where to a parent you're a dotted outline.
Missing. Heart-stirred and rummaging
through suburban bars. Think about it.
How much of your laughter ever made it out
of those dark and humble markets?

So, what did my father really have to go on?
Those summers on the front steps? His sad golden boy
leaning against the stucco with a cup of instant ramen?

A sunset?

LOGIC

Kid, I want you to know
I did walk through the doors
I was told would change me for good,

but anyone can tell you I was
never any good at harmonizing
progress with the mist of memory.

I'd had so much, but the gardens
down the street all kept on
blooming. So many of us
gone, but lovers still
showed up at my front door.

I had to stop apologizing for that.

I couldn't synchronize the ticking
of my watch with the tolling of the church
your grandpa took me to on Sixth Street.

So what else could I do
but tell myself what I'd been hearing
was someone playing with its bells.

SUMMER, YOU'RE A BONEYARD

and you used to be The Richard Bey Show
and my sister's spaghetti. Under a friar plum tree,
a simplified reading of "The Argonautica."
You kept me full and entertained. I was that kind
of round child. Gorging on what was left over.
I didn't want a real burden, my own ship or story.
I didn't want to go on ahead. I didn't want to
have to reverse into you. Into your apparatus.
I never wanted nostalgia. We used to know each other,
remember? Dry. Humid. Dry. Humid.
Not. Humid. Dry. Humid. Humid. Dry. Dry.
Why did we have to pry open our patch of dirt?
Why couldn't you always be acid wash
or those I CAN'T DRIVE 55 posters at the swap meet
or sunglasses. I never wanted to lay questions around
you. What if he takes another this year? What if
he's difficult to talk my way out of? What if he eats me
only half-alive? What if all he is in his beach bum
orange is ghosts clothespinned to the laundry line?

BACHELOR'S PRAYER TO THE CONSTELLATION AQUARIUS

We are down here and most of us are done
rifling through the night. We are down here
and what is public has begun to shutter. Some of us
may have said love before we were to say love,
and Father, tonight I too may have faced humiliation.
But there's relief in the cool air of this offramp.
In the stream and in this awkward shiver. There's relief
'cause I look up. Way up and there you are
in the dark like tomorrow, so blurred and so open.

BACHELOR

Useless now turning to thoughts of winning
the day back. Outside, the dirt gray backwash
against the curbs—how sad it is to brush away
the empties. Partner, wrangler, lover, you
who may by now be on the other side
of Broadway, I don't feel like making up
a new apology. Not when that kiss
was unavoidable. Not when this heat
and this man's words hit like Jupiter-8 chords
and not when a new chord has been known
to bring entire cities back. Think of
blood in the body, of all the hungry ghosts
lined up at the edge of the sun's western copper.

GOLD CHAIN

More often than I should, the herringbone.
Forgotten on nightstands. Returned to
reassure me that I am the girth
they all want to hand to the sculptor,
the mouth, and every word
that is a staircase to a lower floor.
Returned to curl in the same drawer
as the medallion that was my mother's.
The one that makes me feel like a bishop
asking the big man for clemency.

WOLF

I'd been stupid enough to think midnight
stood still everywhere, but you
smelled like bar smoke and rubbed-off
aftershave. At one a.m. you came to me
and said you wanted to stay up
and count all the things we were
free of. Our shirts came clean off,
then our black jeans by the nightstand.
How tall and alike. How firm
and clear to say one thing and mean
one thing. I matched your growl
and exhale, how they resolved in a kiss.
I was learning how to be your man
and the competition. I was learning
how to leave and be left
and never have to get used to the space.

SINGLES

for Danielle

We weren't wild things. Other than the silver
you lobbied against that I still keep in my ears
we left that old year nearly unharmed. So what
is the point in all of this remembering?
All this talk and this putting ourselves back there.
What's left of us in those places anyway,
and what use is that summer and its spine
of graduated errors? The jilted fiancé
who almost won you back. The stud
who left me without breakfast that Fourth of July.
The diamond cut of the earth and the slow
discount furnishing of our bad apartments.
Is it that we were together? It's humor, maybe.
Us. Together. On our tiny balconies, lynx-eyed,
standing on the backs of men, still struggling to see out.

HAPPY NOW?

A whole year I had nightmares
of waiting at the end of the aisle

the suit was gray and skinny
it was hot and I was mad

I hated the lilies for runwaying
the way like yellow lanterns

I hated white I wanted cream
I was thick thick as wool

thick in the same old places
and I could smell it so close by

that median where the mallow
always bloomed that watering hole

by the mechanic's shop I didn't
envy youth I would never fear age

I wanted: to wear navy to have a single
orange hang over a single neighbor's fence

for this city to call me its only son
to flatter me in its same old language

NOCTURNE

The kind with the tv on and three men waiting for my call.
For two of them I described a group of stars in homily.
For one I rattled off the late-night movies that kept me
up as a child. I described to him the midnight club scenes.
The sailors and the anchors mounted to the walls.
Smoke in the eyes. A knife thrown from across the room
to warn off a competing lover. As a child I gawked
at the neon. A bowl of leftover stew on my lap. I wanted
the night with a spoon put up for some distance. I sat. I watched.
The bottle untouched. The last table before the dance floor.

I CAN'T SETTLE ON ONE FIGURE
FOR A SUNSET

But one day inside a bar I called it sweet.

Flames were painted on the walls. There was a little light
in the frosted windows.

I like a lover to call me sweet sometimes. Sweet in the abstract.
Sweet in its expanded form. Sweet like calling sweet a figure.
The figure of a dime-sized pendant, a stick of gum folded up
in a wallet, a smooth-shaped number of ex-lovers.

I was sweet on what was left of the light that day.
I was sweet on it, and I was sweet.

Sweet like reading a good sentence for the first time very slowly.

Marcus, Robert, Matías, and Jesse all took turns
grinding orange slices into the lip of my glass.

GIGOLO / LEXICON

It's an art asking when a husband will be home.

Asking rhetorically if it isn't true
that fear was the first
of mankind's purities.

I have never really cared for purity.

In school I bit down hard on the corners
of *The Pilgrim's Progress*
and every coming-of-age novel
I was assigned. My English
teacher once told me my name
sounded like strength
with a sense of humor.

Humor, she said, and handed me
an over-xeroxed *Mostellaria*.

She told me to clamp down
on language. That I'd need it.
And I have. Quite often.

POEM

What it is is hunkering down inside of a small house
with my father and my mother. My body and the middle
of the month of February. Watching the blooming
of the arrayán from my bedroom window and listening
to the water main. Standing real still in the shower.
Still like water that serves as a mirror. The first mirror
in the history of mirrors, like my father and my mother.
Standing real still in the mirror. Trying to figure out
if there's a pattern in my chest hair, measuring
the quadrants of my face to keep my mustache straight.

BACHELOR

I've grown up so hard
the old home is home
again. So hard I don't know
where any of my exes are.

A young family moves in
across the street, and I say
I know this story: Long ago
both my parents lived
here waiting for their stray cats
to come in.

All hours, a door opening. At all hours
a light in some eggshell room.

Look at the driveway now.
Whittled down to the lone white
Honda in the partial shade
of the few constants: the tree, the gable.

I can't keep straight all the ways
time has scared me or should
scare me. I take the trash out
on Mondays, sun still up.

At night I brush my teeth
and it gets quiet,
but I sometimes wake
the baby birds that nest
out in the yard.

BEACH TOWN

I will never live here with you
or anyone else. The neighbors
walk out to the shore,
to the corner store. Plunge
into the sea to undo the concrete.
I don't care about their views
on personal freedom, on love.
I no longer need the dark
or the one blind eye of promises.
All I need this town to be today
is your apartment.
Absolutes. The stone fruit
the man in 26B dropped off
for you. Your blonde hair.
The soft coral. The saltwater tank.

MOTHER

When she returned, she cut the lilies down
at their creases, the soft spot of the neck
that had given in. As expected,
those by the leaking gnarl of hose survived.
The backyard tomato vine, she knew
before she left, would owe its life to the gardener.

Find me a perfect son. One in all of history.

I kept the canaries happy, didn't I?
Sifted the seed and wedged the bread
they share with the sparrows
between the bars of their cage.

I painted the walls back to white.
I call the color 1993.
All day, I whistle around the house
like my father used to.

I want her to understand I know
that this is what we have left of that love:

This shadow that also doubles as its spirit.
This dry and timid incompleteness.
This failure to move back into the world.
This wanting to move out into the world and failing.

UNTITLED

My father's friend is dead. The one who owned the produce warehouse.
I don't really know if that warehouse is how he wants to be remembered,
but that's how I remember him. The rolling door. The lettuce bins.
How do I know what the dead appreciate? My father is gone too, and
even there I mostly deal in educated guesses. He loved every city at five
in the morning. He missed driving in the dark when his eyes started to
fail. And the living, what do they think of what I choose to focus on?
My brother and my sisters. My father's friend's stable of sons. How do I
know if what I say will be enough or sound the way I mean it to? Even
here. This should be Atotonilco and the early workweek sun. Sound
of brooms on a wet sidewalk. A handshake over a cold cast iron scale.

EL MONJE BLANCO

An actor said the word víspera. I asked my mother what it meant.
I wore a white shirt. Wore no cologne. No gold.

My men. My men had all gone pale. Had pleated into themselves.
I sat on my own couch. The actors on television cried,
and I asked my mother, too, if she thought I'd ever suffered.

    It is not suffering.
    You wait but always know that you are waiting.
    Above your room is the night.
    You hear the world.
    You hear it winding.

I am beautiful, an actor admitted, *I have seen myself in the rivers*.
Víspera, my mother said, the eve of something. A holy day. A drop of rain.

YUZUKO FINDS OUT WHAT THE REST OF THE FAMILY ALREADY KNEW

I knew it wouldn't be the night of the breakup
that would show you who I was.
It would be the day he and I were mended
and I came home with a fresh cut
and flowers for the altar and food for the dog
when you'd see that I was someone who would
only be with you when I had someone else to love.

ESTOY AQUÍ

for Abdul

What you feel—it is the breath of the next world.
I know; I have been here with the door
and this window open all day.

And the next world has found its place
again in this kitchen, and it is still my father
telling me the sky is clearing and it is still
the avocado tree in the backyard for decades
recklessly giving itself away.

It is a song that's been the pillar of poem
after poem. And it is the day
after the day you said you loved me.

You know, my mother always warned me
never to mistake a house, not even hers,
for the house of divine providence,
but you are here with your palms
over my palms and your face
almost feels like a miracle.

HERCULES IN HIS BOYFRIEND'S HAIR

Waves, and in a dark so forgiving it doesn't have to be midnight.
I tell you waves even though in the older myths we are told curls.

I ask you to believe *me*, lover. Think
of the other translations we've found permissible: Our hero played

by that famous bodybuilder. To get the job he fudged the truth
about his stage experience. The chariot scene on the streets

of New York was shot without a permit. Earlier, that Claymation
nightmare where both our men were in their thirties, probably

classically trained and, I think, British. So, here the boyfriend's hair
is the tide, but the fathers are still immortal and long dead. You see

this isn't some revolutionary departure. We start in a hotel room
with our hero running his fingers through the dark. Gold-plated

box chain, a Hawaiian shirt hanging off a writing desk. A blunt
and common scene and message. This myth, like everything

else in the realm of love, can be stripped down to the vulnerable.
To admitting we need someone to bear our arrows, guard our bow.

A FANTASY

On what is sometimes still called love and lust.
On those red minerals.
On the bee and boxwood and the 55 Freeway.
On summer and its officers.
On your climb up the Comfort Inn stairwell.
On my age. On God and the smoke shop.
On this room and the obfuscation of heaven.
On that. On that embroidered comforter

I sat down. I removed my shoes.

CONCLUSION

I made what I wanted to make out of love then.

On a bed I sat next to you. In a movie,
Pedro Armendáriz talked in circles
about the color in his lover's eyes.
It was August. The actor's own eyes glowed.
I didn't tell you that he's killed in the last act.
I turned the movie off. That was our love in those days.
That, and later the blue dive across the street.
Friday night and its yellow booth.

BACHELOR

I think my brother a gray pragmatist
just as he thinks me stuck
in Cupid's pink revolving door.

He asks if I'm okay, and I know
he wants to hear I've reconciled
every paradigm I've tried.
That I now lived in protracted
thanksgiving and nothing else.

Hands his daughter to me,
and it means *She'll one day ask about all this.*
You should want her to believe that you had everything
and asked for nothing.

How will you cover up the mixed-up playboy in love with love
those first few weeks? How you show off to your lovers.

My brother says that showing off
can be another form of begging.

BACHELOR'S PRAYER TO THE LOVE OF HIS LIFE

You who insists on marrying
the earth to its next day
have got me all mixed up.
Thinking of night
as a bridge, as some sort
of present for the groom.
I'm sitting up, dressed
in black, trying to defend the idea
of this house as a presbytery,
but I'm drifting in and out
of sleep. I am drifting in and out
of sleep and you are everywhere.

SON

It is raining. Here and in my mother's dream.
The house there is quiet.
The rain flows into the verdolaga.
I am not forty-five. I am a few weeks old
and the house is in disrepair. My mother
worries and says worry has never known
how to live only inside of a dream.
The water will come through the rafters.
Will fall right where my baby is sleeping.

THEORY

All afternoon, and up to their curfew, planes
flew out of the airport next door.
Our room was paid for. It was spring
and I couldn't stop thinking
about that sunny Whitman quote
over the couch next to the bed.

I said it was a big blockheaded thing to think
you should always face forward.
Over and over, I looked out the window
at our parked cars under the oak.

I sat through March. I sat through April
like a fat cardinal. I scolded you
about Whitman. Said I thought the lines old
and overripe and obvious, and now—

what I think now is all my life I've paid
in transpositions.

What I think now is that in spring,
when you still wanted to, we should have married.

NOCTURNE

The light above the stove in this kitchen is never turned off.
It's bright enough to warm something in the skillet by.
There we are, the skillet and me, at one in the morning.
Odd hours these days, this house.

I have read that in the Middle Ages people often slept
in two short shifts. What they called a first and second sleep.
It is mentioned in old courthouse records.
It shows up somewhere in *The Canterbury Tales*.

Maybe that is what I have returned to.

Every night I sink twice into what was. Two sets of dreams.

I show up to my grandparents' house forty-five and unannounced.
I sell jicamas on the road with my nephew and my father.

The hours in between I imagine I use in the same way as those before me.
For these small, warm tasks. To feed myself what I lacked during the day.
For small prayers and even smaller declarations.

THE RUNNER

The house now at some distance, I kneel
to tie my laces in the middle of the street.
The middle of winter. The early morning.
Puddles obedient and clean as mirrored glass.

To my mother it seems an odd thing.
This running for running's sake.
Strange, she says, Leaving your bed
and leaving a kitchen warm
in its cooked guayabas and its cinnamon.

Strange as when she first heard me pronounce
the words track and frost and American holly.
First watched this country code
both language and kinetic custom into me.

It is important to know I was mostly blank
when I was brought here. Important too
that I wasn't completely. Each morning
I convert Santa Ana's miles to kilometers
for her, kilometers to landmarks in Jalisco:

A warmup from the stone of our old house
to La Casa de Plata. A race from our plaza
to the western borders of Tototlan.

POEM

What did I love? Being able to touch
all four walls. Pressing on the words
hair and hunk and grain until they gave
me what I wanted. What I loved was
counting out the almonds in my palm.
At times ignoring the steps of the men
in the attic, even though I loved them
and whatever else I carried up there.
Dad's alarm clock. My brother's boogie
boards. All but one of the plaid shirts
I owned. I loved them. I loved that I
carried them up there. That I shaved
after I took my lunch on Wednesdays.
That there was silver in the blade.

SANTA ANA AT MIDNIGHT

I will never be able to have this town
wrapped up like I want it.
There are things here sleeping so down deep
that you'll never stop feeling for them.
Three video stores walking distance
from my childhood home—posters
and black plastic bones now buried
under the ground. The old neighbors
and their voices—a street marked
up and across with everything
they ever said. *I held all the keys
that were made here. I wanted to own something,
but I never did.* Both satisfaction and need
once had a body, though not always
their own body. Not everything is resolved
like it was in nineties films.
We have the wreathed walnut door
behind which our story ends and begins,
but there are streets with their mouths still
open. Streets over which some fathers still
float back to their graves unanswered.
Grocery store circulars left behind
on bus benches. Rafters. And the cold.

NOVENA

I am too far from our old church
and its courtyard and priest I am closer

to my mother and the television
and this Noé Murayama monologue

I want to remember and repeat
the words in his voice

to imagine my father listening to me
in that movie theater in the 50s

the theater he said was a church
to him for a time he had a brother

close by like I have a brother close
to me now the other night a friend

said our two voices sounded alike
and we smiled and said our father

and I repeated my brother's name and
he said his daughter's name all evening

this is how far we are from our old church
these are our prayers to the dead now

CHRISTMAS CARD

The edges I would like for you to gild
in plastic. Holly, heaven and nature
all from a First Street dollar store.
Above, the sad winter sun and my brother,
not yet forty, guiding his daughter
from every sharp thing in the yard,
from fooling with our mother's canaries,
to where I'm standing. Maybe wondering
from where the instincts of a childless person
come. Just look at me. The brother. The uncle.
Despite the loss and the wild untethered
weight of calling the shots to my own
growing up, I offer my flannelled arms
and joy like a sudden umbel
of butterfly weed. Now the busy street
and its modified mufflers, now
the house and my body and her body
weigh less than a handful of seed.

POEM

for Diane

She told me to make it
to turn it around to bathe
the old haystacks in silver
tinsel made to represent snow
snow on our patched-up houses
on the memory of someone
who loved us or taught us
someone who wrote a good one
called "Christmas Night"
She told me to hold it and to listen
if not snow then rain at least
rain can be a late factory shift
the stars or that parking lot you like
on that street where you told me
the good burger joint was
McFadden named after a man
and you don't remember why rain
on that street where you grew up
there where you are where you don't
know the first thing about snow

DECEMBER

I don't want anything to turn. I don't
think it needs to. The heat works.
The skylight again has stopped leaking.
I used to read everything under that
skylight. Nothing got out. Nothing got in.
As a child, I was sure Hawthorne wrote
the devil only in the trees outside of town.

I CAN'T SETTLE ON ONE FIGURE FOR A SUNSET

The fiction class suggestion of an old red cloak.
The soul becoming orange. Honest and masculine
prayer. Sugar. Insulin the body makes or doesn't make.

The medicine I organize in front of my mother's dresser
in this room where sunset used to be a small TV
bought hot out of a yellow Datsun. Tallulah Bankhead
playing herself on *I Love Lucy*. Tallulah Bankhead, a black widow
villain fighting Batman in a rerun. My brother next to me.

Knowing the impossibility of reversal.
Not knowing whether you will get back the dirt road
or the unobstructed view of the river. Looking up from the pills
and my dead father's cologne. The soul becoming orange.

CONCLUSION

Sweet boy, with your lens, you saw.

A man who told me he, too, could see
in my face every man and boy I'd ever been.
His search for tenderness. His use of its edge
against me. The weeks when I woke up
and I woke up in his mirror, plain as bedstraw.
The seven-a.m. living room and the warmth
of the concern on my brother-in-law's brow.
That Thursday morning in the kitchen
when my brother and his wife asked me point blank
if I'd been lonely. Lonely. The plain way
they said lonely and the way I often say lonesome
when I want to sound like a cowboy. You saw
the grain and the yellowing grass and my face
in the same light as the house and the local hotel
and its key. The dark dissipating. The frame
of the window and the sun coming up
the color of American bittersweet.

RELICS

all that broken ceramic behind the town church.
The wing, the crown, the sword, lily and lamp.
It's embarrassing sometimes, the way I worry
there won't be time to get every little piece right.
The railroad flare in my father's eyes. The boy
sleepwalking with one hand in his brother's pocket.
The train they called La Guayaba and 1973
when electricity came to San Isidro.
When my mom's family traded in their old flat iron
for a coconut. The sunset and clay time
of traveling merchants who sometimes stole
the silverware right from under your nose.
The eyes of a seer kept warm by the wood-burning
stove. Today the eyes of the friend who traded me in
for Jesus and the horns in the OutKast song
your father played for me in his black Ford.
The way the clasp of my gold chain never sits
behind my nape, and how I use all these pieces
and don't use the big noun around you, Baby.
To ask you to pay attention. To tell you
the ferries are being feathered away from the shore.

BACHELOR

My niece Casandra trusts me
when I tell her I am happy.
When I describe the wind
blowing through the juniper
in this parking lot
as Christmas-in-the-desert cold.

Across the street, heat lamps and white
canopies shield a backyard wedding party.
Across from us her parents lean into themselves
for warmth.

I've had love that has run parallel to that.
Made two good homes with two good men.
Made some small and crooked talisman
of them, although ultimately nothing
that has now come to protect me.

I am not a match for anyone,
and I make Casandra smile
because instead of saying that
I say that life has paid me well
but it has paid only in silver.

LA CARABINA DE AMBROSIO

I've named the stray cat that tries to get at the canaries
El Destino. This last month I've been half cynic,
half television special. My mother, who still believes
improvised altars are lightning rods for a miracle,
says the humor—the good that has returned to me—
is grace, and sometimes I want to agree with her,
but who these days really remembers the definition
of grace, or every one of its definitions and then
each one's reach and breadth? These years have not
been years made to be sure of anything. We wonder
if El Destino will forget the birds if we stop taking
the cage out to the yard. We both think it unlikely.
Just about everything now is in some way unrelenting,
and the birds are no good to anyone locked up inside.

EPILOGUE

Man. Son. Old Uncle. You say you want to
keep yourself in this winter forever.
Save yourself the trouble. Save your voice too.
I know you're not the rain. I know you aren't
the new year. You can sleep. For you
I'll keep the vase of holly in the corner,
the tree up well past Three King's Day.

CONCLUSION

It is small, this house. My father is gone.

I hear the tinkling bells of his sheep—
a line from a Rossetti poem
I keep on my nightstand. And I do.
Hear them sometimes.
When my mother shuffles from room
to room. Like hymn and memory.
Verse and road away from Bethlehem.
In pale blue lines through every hallway.

BACHELOR

for Maximiliano

What do you want to hear first?

Dinners alone I often sat with my back to the street.

Once in a Greek restaurant,
where I faced a bearded cook
who winked at me, a bakery display
with four kinds of baklava.

That is what sometimes passed for love.

Faces and gestures and beards.
Numbers and numbers and numbers.

Your great-grandmother had a habit of saying
she could write a book *this big*.
And that was just about one man.

What would my book be?

The night and the overuse of the romantic poets?
The temporary loss of command that was
always a handful of store-bought narcissus?

Devotion? To my sister, your mother, maybe,
but what I usually did with devotion
was stir it out of its cup, like a child
with the milk he'd been given.

I am not a virtuous example, not like your grandfather,
who absent his father brought the village priest with him
when he asked for your grandmother's hand,
who cared for his mother as a single and a married man.

I was not big enough for that. I closed myself off
to one kind of love. And what filled
the awkward amount of space that was left?
Certainly, a type of cartoon hedonism, but also truth.
In me telling you this, some purpose.

NOCTURNE

This one's a painting of me in dark blues, and one of the blues
is the color of the storm clouds in Carrington's
The Temptation of Saint Anthony. There is the suggestion
of light in my eyes, my top buttons are undone and silver.
I am moving over the LA river on the Sixth Street Bridge.
Movement in a painting can be created using rhythm.
Rhythm can be a frequently recalled memory: a 90s episode
of *Love Connection* where an Orange County man
is called an Orange County boy and is berated by his date
for his small-town mindset, for being afraid to park
his midnight blue Mustang on a downtown street.
I was taught that for every work of art there is always
some strange, expositional story we can tell about the artist.
Some obsessive mindset. Something tight but warped.
The moon is in the painting, but the moon was not painted
with the purpose of illumination. The moon is secrecy.
The bridge is not lit up. Its copper wire's been stolen.

CONCLUSION

It's hard luck.

My plane is landing, and I swear the moon
has held this exact crescent for days.
The one night we spent together
you shut the curtains on it.
Moved my chain aside with your mouth.
Reminded me what those hours were.
Full and all we'd ever have.
That room was not my home.
What passes now below me is.
I will always want to give it to you. Our share
of the interstate and the courthouse. The canyon.
The one military hangar left after the fire.

END IT ON THIS

What did I do. Did I fly—did I powerlift—did I

draw. Did I draw myself and my house and my father.

Did the house have a green trim. Did I call the green trim

Walden Pond. Did I play you. Did I buy you lunch

by the ocean. Did I walk you around

with my index finger in your mouth. Did I time the kiss.

Was I paying attention to the song in the background

all along. Was that it. Was that the point of it all.

That I fell in love. That I wrote it down on a parking lot ticket.

THERE WAS ALSO THE MATTER OF
HOW HE SAW HIMSELF

The aging sitcom hunk
All / American / Fall / Leaf /
Scripted / Love / Handled /
Kitchen / Counter / Sunset

The widow's bachelor son
[Beef stew boiling]
[Rows of folded crew socks]

The bishop falling asleep
at his desk every night
In every cloister all is well
that ends well, and all is well.

The boy who is now nearly a lie
: an open field, another town,
a wildflower growing there.

BACHELOR

Second to God he said he loved the way I kissed him.
Second to God, and I feared he'd make himself sick
on my body. My body was an unchecked thing.
Generous. It sat beside him. It smiled. That made it
perfect. That body with a whole history missing.
That body built up from a plastic timeline.
I stopped telling one story to all of my lovers.
Of being a child. Of being kept out of a party
because I'd not brought a present. Every story
is an open ask of its audience. I did not want to ask
for pity. *Second to God,* he said, and when he'd opened
the door, I'd only done what I'd done my entire life—
I'd walked in. My pockets stuffed with unpeeled oranges.

MOSTELLARIA

After years in a holy land, the father returns in traveling clothes.
Wallet and business cards and nail clipper in his front pockets.
He returns to rumors of a haunted house. He returns to set his
house in order, to find his errant son missing. *The word errant
in its ancient use means a search for adventure. Adventure is
justifiable.* That was the son speaking stage left behind a closed
door. The father has entered stage right. The entire audience
has longed to see the father. Longed to see him eat at his table
again. Longed for the long-overdue accounting. They all want
the house repaired—the son, wide-eyed and dense as a brick wall,
set straight—the fruit trees trimmed and the garden soil turned.
In the play, the father speaks to the son through a small series
of arbitrators. He doesn't share one proper scene with the son.

SUNDAY MORNING

Yeah, sure, I've also been one acquainted with the night.
Everyone here in the masa line has. If clothes can spell out
heartbreak, our clothes spell out heartbreak. A leopard
overcoat. Mascara stains on microsuede. A crooked hat.
My hoodie over me like the pelt of the Nemean Lion.
This too is a trial. I too have held myself accountable. I'm here,
and I guess this is what it takes to prove I still know love.
My mother, my sister, and the dog who were able to remain asleep.
This town and these same old faces. This tired, tight-lipped man
leaning on the yellow wall who is almost the night on his own.
He's right, you know, there isn't much left that you can say.
The sun's coming back up. Most of us already know what
the sky is playing out. Only the ignorant still need to speak.

MORNING SONG

When I was a kid, I looked through piles of burnt garbage
for empty perfume bottles. This is the tinkling of the glass.
Every morning my mother gently reminds her canaries
to pay for their food. This is that and the canaries and also
the soft sound of my mother's sewing machine when I
was twenty-three and found myself living back home. Little
bee on a metal coil on the roof of a small wooden house
that my niece pulls back and then lets fly. The little house
and the hooves of my nephew's plastic horse on the living
room glass. Rustle of my leather vest that is not a cowboy vest.
Gunsmoke on tv and the dry fields and the voices of the actors
who are all long gone. My father had a strong, joyful voice
and a funny way of saying golly! With a long pause
between the syllables. This is my dad saying gol-
ly! and the hooves of my nephew's plastic horse on the living.

GREENLIGHT

All it was was a parking lot. A parking lot in a dream.
In Texas. Where neither of us was. Where I'd never been.
I don't like bringing up dreams in conversation, but I said it:
A dream, and I drove my truck with you next to me.
I said things that lovers say when running errands around town.
A comment on the price of ice cream. A question about the curry.
Nothing much happened. Some dirt. Some sun. Some tread.
I awoke the next morning unchanged. A man used to saying
words and watching the world react. It's simple. My life right now
is full but not complex. I rarely remember what I've dreamt.
I write, but sometimes write and somehow find that I dislike
associations. Dislike them almost as much as I dislike questions.
Like *is all connection impermanent?*
Like *which one of us is going to teach the other that?*

CONCLUSION

I was dense and good-natured.

I wore my checkered shirt tucked in and took
as love the parcel you brought over our hills.
I said no to receiving the hills as a metaphor.
I said no to equation and philosophy.
I wore my checkered shirt tucked in.
You said rest your handsome head.
You smoothed my hair. When you left,
I was alone. I was something silent in your mind.

CHRISTMAS CARD

Fortunate, those who have been called to dinner.
The sky went cold early today, the sycamores quiet.
Nothing wants to sway in this dark.

I thank the walls of this house and the west window.
I am consoled. I've managed language for so long,
lonely doesn't have to mean lonely anymore.

I have convinced myself that it means everything
to have recovered by winter some of what I gave away.
The dry laurel and the aviators. What I kept hanging
upside down from gates and rearview mirrors.

Any man who's left outside can claim or level what he wants.
Tonight, the door's been locked for hours.
Tonight, I've no calls left to make.

NOCTURNE

The core of this house has gone dark,
but I can see by the light of his lamp
that the neighbor boy keeps at his schoolwork.

I am not a boy. I learned a long time ago
the things for which we reserve panic.
For most others there are only two options:
you do or you pay.

As a young man, I often cried to my father
for an old answer. The answer for the overdue loan,
for the heart falling apart or the heart disappearing.
En esta vida hay remedio para todo menos la muerte.

This darkness is nothing, a switch that needs to be switched.
There are worse things than the cold in the backyard.
This house is mine, and the night had so far been kind.

There is whiskey in my coffee.
I have a jacket lying around.
The lights around my father's altar will soon be lit.

SON

My mother is in the kitchen, and in the living room

> Anna Lætitia Barbauld's husband drowns
> himself in a river built to bring water to London.

> An older Luis Aguilar sings in a turmeric suit;
> his mustache has been dyed two shades too dark.

> Aguilar was nicknamed El Gallo Giro.
> He once starred in a movie called *Los Cuatro Juanes*
> and played the Juan called "Juan sin Miedo."

I am afraid of everything. The mind unfastening and the body
giving up.

> Barbauld, in one of her last poems, asked
> life to choose its own time to leave her,
> asked it not to say good night, but in some
> greater clime bid her good morning.

It's brave, giving yourself up like that.

> Hopeful, the expectation of the great eye-
> opening somewhere in another world.

I sometimes remember that sermon.

> Sitting on Sundays with half the good
> people in this city, next to my poor father.

74

Now that he's gone, how am I expected to answer that call
to silence and to sudden dispossession and to granite? To forget

the open nightstand drawers,
his keys hidden in teapots and the mass
of safes with combinations never written down

his grandchildren sleeping and my mother in the kitchen
with the Walmart clock above her

the one with the painted roses and the scrollwork
that reads *All things are possible if you believe.*

I CAN'T SETTLE ON ONE FIGURE
FOR A SUNSET

But in a dream it was a ranch, and in that dream
I understood that every hectare was our bloodline.
It was a Sunday, and my mother scolded me.
She said I didn't need a horse to shave my face
and get to mass. I sat outside the way dust sits
on wooden steps or on a prayerbook,
and the light hit the outlying branch of an oak.

YUZUKO AND HER UNCLE AT SUNDOWN

The electric razor at my cheek beneath the orange tree.
Me and the razor and you and the orange tree
and the worn book in your hands in the hand mirror
and the past behind us. I said the past was tall
as Minoan horses. The sun and the orange glow
in the yard. I said I liked the old Greeks best
when they described ivory and the gold you could shape
to adorn it. When they wrote ivory and gold.
Ivory and gold in hooves and wreaths. Stretches of them.
Long forward-facing roads of them. Ivory and gold
shaped into battle and deluge. Shaped into the loss of hope.
Into myths and into people answering their own prayers
and questions. I said I answered my own question.
About hope and facing forward. I asked you to find me
the story about the head honcho threatened by a raging flood.
About the bird that guided him to the top of the mountain.
A little bird. A mountain that had always been there.

BACHELOR

I haven't changed the curtains in my room
since I moved in. A deep and a deeper blue.
All of my lovers have seen them.

My last lover was young. He kept
pomade in my right vanity drawer.
When I told him that my father died,
he didn't have a single word for loss.

Say family. Say four walls. Say the hum of bees.
Say it is a long trip on horseback. A justification.
Say son. Say husband. Say archbishop. Say night.

I have taught all of my lovers how to speak.
How to say I want to open my eyes
inside any house you live in. How to say I want to see
the sun and then the sun set in your city.

I have taught all of my lovers how to write.
The lamp that sits in the corner of my room is dim.
I have taught all of them how to describe it.

ACKNOWLEDGMENTS

Academy of American Poets, "Summer, You're a Boneyard"

Night Heron Barks, "Divorce with Pulled-Back Curtain and Electrical Wiring" (Published as "Window Shades")

Citric Acid, "Husband (Despite the times we couldn't decide)," "Bachelor (Useless now turning to thoughts of winning)," "Bachelor's Christmas Card," "Sunday Morning," "The Runner," "I Can't Settle on One Figure for a Sunset (Though sometimes I'd like for it to be the Willow Thicket)"

Anacapa Review, "Nocturne (The kind where the horses have been hitched to the trees)"

Bracken, "Cienega"

Honey Literary, "Hercules in His Boyfriend's Hair"

Heimat Review, "Estoy Aquí"

Adroit Journal, "Son (It is raining)," "Theory," "Untitled," "Husband (After that night)"

Quarterly West, "Baritone"

like a field, "Yuzuko at Evening Mass," and "Happy Now?"

Mānoa Journal, "Nocturne (The light above the stove)," "Novena," "El Monje Blanco," and "Bachelor's Prayer to the Constellation Aquarius"

Poetry International Online, "Morning Song" and "La Carabina de Ambrosio"

Villain Era Lit, "Bachelor (In one of the black and white films)," "End It on This," "Gigolo/Lexicon"

Thank you to Edward and everyone at FlowerSong Press.

Diane
DTK. SSP. AAD. PFU. +tax.

Dorothy
"Like, no amor please."

James
Libra x Aquarius 4ever

Thank you to my family and friends.

About the Author

Gustavo Hernandez is the author of the poetry collection *Flower Grand First* (Moon Tide Press, 2021). In January 2024, Hernandez was appointed Poet Laureate of Orange County, California. He was born in Jalisco, Mexico and was raised in Santa Ana, California, where he still resides.

It's a chancy job, but it makes a man watchful…and a little lonely.

—Matt Dillon,
Gunsmoke

FLOWERSONG
PRESS

FlowerSong Press nurtures essential verse
from, about, and throughout the borderlands.
Literary. Lyrical. Boundless.

Sign up for announcements about
new and upcoming titles at:

www.flowersongpress.com

www.ingramcontent.com/pod-product-compliance
Lightning Source LLC
Chambersburg PA
CBHW020757130626

46554CB00006B/2227